Rough Mu

Published by bluechrome publishing 2006

2 4 6 8 10 9 7 5 3 1

First published in Great Britain in 2006 by
bluechrome publishing
PO Box 109,
Portishead, Bristol. BS20 7ZJ

www.bluechrome.co.uk

A CIP catalogue record for this book is available from the British
Library

ISBN 1-904781-48-9

Rough Music

Patrick B. Osada

Dedications

To all the battling people of Warfield, trying hard to save the integrity of their village and the surrounding countryside.

To Lynn : for her inspiration and encouragement; to my family for their interest and support.

Acknowledgements

Twenty six poems from this collection have already appeared in the following magazines, anthologies and websites or won prizes in poetry competitions :
Acumen, British Isles Poetry Anthology, Berkshire Literary Festival Anthology, Coffee House Poetry, Decanto, Eclipse, Embroidering Eternity Anthology, Envoi, www.footballpoets.org, www.interpoetry.com, Liverpool Festival Poetry Competition 2006, Nature in Motion Anthology, www.othervoicespoetry.org, Ottakar's & Faber Ninth Annual Poetry Competition, Poetry Cornwall, Poetry Monthly, Poetry on the Lake Competition 2006, Places Within Reach (Anthology), Reach, South, The Coffee House, www.quillandink.netfirms.com, Weyfarers…

To the editors and judges concerned, a special "thank you."

Other poems from *Rough Music* have also appeared on my own website, **www.poetry-patrickosada.co.uk**

Introduction

Warfield is a semi rural Parish of thirteen hamlets and settlements. Mentioned in the Doomsday Book, Warfield was originally a Saxon settlement and the hunting grounds for Saxon Kings.
One of the most colourful incidents from Warfield's history occurred in 1874 when the villagers went mob handed to the local home of Lord Ormathwaite to... *"play rough music"*- a noisy demonstration of disapproval at the ill-treatment of his wife.

The rural character of the area changed little over the years until the development of the nearby "New Town" by the Bracknell Development Corporation, set up by the Government in 1949. Since then there has been a constant battle to preserve Warfield against the threat of developers and planners. Gradually the tentacles of tarmac have extended out from Bracknell's concrete heart, carrying suburbia deeper into the surrounding countryside.

In 1983, under pressure from central Government, Berkshire County Council identified North East Bracknell as a location for 4000 new homes.
There followed five years of vigorous campaigning by the councils of Warfield Parish and the Borough, local community groups and the newly formed Northern Parishes Action Group. Their demands, that no new houses be built on countryside between Warfield and Bracknell, was overruled by Nicholas Ridley, Secretary for State, in 1988.
At that time Warfield had a population of a little over 1,700 (about the same as it was at the time of the Black Death, 1345 - 1351). Today (2006) it has risen to over 8,500, with the greater portion of this new population living in housing estates at the southern end of the Parish on land that previously marked the boundaries of parish and town.

In 1997 the new Draft Regional Planning Guidance for the South East of England was announced with recommendations for a massive increase in house building in Berkshire...With little in the way of reusable *brownfield* sites available, countryside was once more under threat and Warfield held its breath…

In the Spring of 2006, responding to directives from Central Government, Bracknell Forest Borough Council announced proposals to build over 10,000 new houses during the next 20 years…Land at Warfield was identified as suitable for use as *"Urban Extensions"* of the Borough - with plans to build 2,500 new homes…
Open countryside at West End / Cabbage Hill has come under threat and, with history seemingly repeating itself, residents have rallied round to form the *KEEP WEST END GREEN CAMPAIGN* and the *WARFIELD ACTION GROUP.*

Like many villages in the South East, Warfield will have to fight to preserve its identity if it is to stave off creeping suburbia. The time for more *Rough Music* is at hand….

The Warfield Poems :

I have been fortunate to be able to spend a great deal of my life living in rural or semi-rural settings. The countryside is important to me and it is, therefore, unsurprising that some of my poetry should have a pastoral theme.

In writing about Warfield, I have attempted to record many everyday and seasonal events of the place where I live. I have been doing this for a number of years and many of the bucolic poems from my earlier collections are also set in this area of Berkshire.
I claim nothing exceptional for Warfield - in terms of history, scenery or wild life. There are places with more tales to tell, areas that are more beautiful, or enjoy exotic or protected flora or fauna. What makes it special for me, my neighbours and the many visitors who come here to walk, ride or cycle is the very fact that much of Warfield remains untouched and unspoilt in an area riven by motorways and so close to the concrete towers of *"New Town"* Bracknell.... It is still possible to be in touch with a life and landscape which has been obliterated by *"planners and developers"* in other less fortunate villages.

Once the bulldozers move in the deer, that have roamed this area for 1,000 years, will move on and with them many other species will leave. With tarmac and streetlights Warfield will be submerged beneath a sea of houses, its traditions and rural atmosphere destroyed...
In the face of *"progress"* and the mindless plans of those happy to see Warfield turned into an *"urban extension"* of Bracknell, I offer up these poems as a celebration of local life and scenery and a warning of what we stand to lose.

Patrick B. Osada
Warfield, July 2006

Contents

The Warfield Poems

WEST END, WARFIELD	13
FROST EPIPHANY	15
JANUARY SUNDAY	16
DEER ON KEITH'S FIELD	17
HEALTH WARNING	18
LARKS ASCENDING	19
UNSEASONAL	20
BERKSHIRE SPRING	21
WHEN DOES WINTER TURN TO SPRING?	22
WILLOW	23
MAGICIANS	24
GREEN AND PLEASANT	25
SALLOW	26
A WALK IN THE COUNTRY	27
FLEDGLING AT WEST END	28
DEATH of the PHEASANT MAN	29
SUMMER RAIN	30
RICHES	31
WARFIELD VISITOR	32
CROWS	33
ON CABBAGE HILL	34
ONE OF THOMPSON'S BOYS	35
SEPTEMBER	36
WINDFALLS	37
HARVEST	38
QUELM LANE	39
OCTOBER MAPLE	40
HORSE CHESTNUTS IN OCTOBER	41
AUTUMN SUNDAY, BERKSHIRE	42
NOT AN ODE TO AUTUMN	43
NOT ALL IT SEEMS	44
AUTUMN FIND	45
WINTER SOLSTICE, WARFIELD	46
LORD ORMATHWAITE'S ROUGH MUSIC	47
ONCE IT'S GONE, IT'S GONE	50

Other Places, Other Faces   **51**
    MOTORWAY EPIPHANY   53
    BLIGHTED SPRING   54
    AT PRACTICE   55
    COTSWOLD VIEW   56
    VIEW WITH A KILL   58
    VALLEY OF THE KITES   59
    ROME   61
    PENSION DAY   62
    PARADOX   63
    THE READING TEST   64
    FROM GRID REFERENCE : 60   (moving west) 65
    DEATH OF A PRINCESS   66
    PAUSE   67
    EASTER MOON   68
    TURNINGS   69
    50s INCIDENT   70
    NO DEVILS OR ANGELS   72
    POETRY MATTERS   73
    BIOGRAPHER   74
    STILL   75
    HER DIAMOND MAN   76
    FEBRUARY 14th.   78
    TONIGHT'S THE NIGHT   79
    PERSONAL EFFECTS   80
    ADAM AS ENTREPRENEUR   81
    SEEING THE LIGHT   83
    THE KNACK   85
    BALLAD FOR THE BELFAST BOY   86
    PUSHING THE BOAT OUT…   89
    SONG (What Progress?)   90
    NOT AUBADE   93
    WILD RANSOMS   95

The Warfield Poems

WEST END, WARFIELD

Where head brass flashed, the sun
Now glints from tractor's screen -
The grandson of the man
Who led a patient team
Roars by, cocooned from larks
And diesel's steady thrum,
His airconditioned cab
Awash with Radio 1.

Still clopping down the lane
These horses are not led -
No longer set in teams,
The working horse is dead.
These are a different breed
More like a family pet,
On Sunday morning rides
They've never broken sweat.

The houses down the lane
Have changed - been much improved,
Extended, modernised
By couples who have moved
Away from urban sprawl.
They breathe the clean fresh air,
Have roses round the door,
But shout, *"Keep West End Green!!"*
When councillors decide,
*"This village needs more homes -
The plan's to urbanise."*

Made more productive now,
This big field's not the same
Haven for mice and game,
Since they grubbed up the hedge.
Where once the village worked
With pitchfork,scythe and 'hook,
Three men and their machines
Soon frighten off the rooks.
They talk on mobile 'phones
And plan the quickest way
To combine, bale and clear
This field in just one day.
The farmer has his plans -
He'd sell the lot today
And welcome new estates
As he lives miles away...

I sit above it all
Watching a changing scene
Where, combine wreathed in dust,
Proves men can't beat machines.
I write where years before
A scythe and billhook stood,
But I don't push a plough -
That's not my livelihood...
Instead I push these words
Across a silver screen.

I watch the sun break through
Where larks have climbed to sing;
Young swallows dart and flash,
A cat strolls down the lane -
As time and man transform
Is all this set to change?...

This poem has grown from an earlier work : "Where head brass flashed" which was
published in 2005. The substantial revision of this piece is a response to the very real threat
that Warfield, and particularly rural land at West End , could be engulfed by a sea of
houses - becoming an "urban extension" of nearby Bracknell .

FROST EPIPHANY

Cold air and moonshine :
White light on grass and trees
Transforms at daybreak -
Solidifies as frost.

Horses like statues -
Frozen to the fields -
Watch in an icy dawn
Where their green world is white.
An orange sunrise -
Framed in distant trees -
Silhouettes the blackthorn hedge.
Everything just gleams :
The pastures glittering,
Each twig and grass blade
Frosted - so complete.

Fast striding up Larks Hill,
Soft ground is summer firm.
Smoky bursts of breath,
Fingers tingle; in my head
A song - the words inquire :
Isn't he the God of creation?
And I am here alone,
Humbled by this glory.

All around is freedom -
Larger than the blue above…

JANUARY SUNDAY

Clinging high in a low tree,
A robin stopped to sing for me
And all the robin world.
Despite the cold and wintry day
It stayed - it did not fly away
And showed no fear of me.
Above my head, above the storm,
Fearless in the greying dawn,
It sang and sang again, *"Rejoice!"*

DEER ON KEITH'S FIELD

Hush!
Snaking between frosted trees
A deer on this frozen field
Tip-toeing
Silent through the fallen leaves.

A deer on this frozen ground
Diamond shoed
Dancing down frosty glitter.

A deer on this frozen field
Twinkle-toed
Prancing passed the winter kale.

A deer over frozen ground
Glassy-glides
Across iced puddled furrows.

Freezing, she takes a final glance -
Disappears into fading light.

HEALTH WARNING

(Down Warfield Lanes)

On murky mornings and grey days
Winter motorists passing through
Hurriedly wind their windows down
To lose their litter in the gloom.
Now, in the first bright glint of Spring,
Like soiled washing in the breeze,
Polythene cloaks the blackthorn hedge.
Along the roadside broken glass
Where fox and badger soon will tread.
Crushed cans and wrappers coat the verge,
Daffodils struggle to be seen -
Smokers die young, the packet says -
But better if it read, *Stay Green!*

LARKS ASCENDING

Beneath a mass of threatening cloud,
I'm wrapped against the forecast snow
As I stride out across *Larks Hill.*
Below, the streaming vehicles groan
Down *Harvest Ride* and on to town.
Yet here, above the traffic's drone,
Comes birdsong over tussocked grass -
Too far to carry from the hedge
But clear above the gusting blast.

Casting about this grassy space
I spot them, dots against the sky,
Riding in air too cold for snow,
Braving this February day.
Whilst others shelter in the hedge,
These tiny crested, feathered scraps
Defy the worst that Winter brings.
Miraculous, daredevil birds
Sing out a challenge and a prayer :
An invocation to the Spring.

UNSEASONAL

Unseasonal the warmth,
This March two seasons coalesce :
Daffodil with bluebell,
Sallow, hazel, primrose, cowslip,
Anemone and celandine.

Everywhere there's bloom and leaf,
High skies invite an early frost
But pairing birds are up to sing.

A sudden wind brings flurried snow,
Strips petals from the blackthorn hedge -
An unexpected mingling :
Confetti for the Spring.

BERKSHIRE SPRING

(Blackthorn & Gorse)

Viewed across the Woodley Road,
Billows of the softest foam
Brilliant dazzle, white on gold.

Looking soft as drifts of snow,
Beautiful like love's sweet face,
Blossom hides thorn's secret place.

WHEN DOES WINTER TURN TO SPRING?

When does Winter turn to Spring?
The signs are there on biting days,
When snowdrops bend to battle wind –
But then this isn't really Spring.

These days are short and wet and grey,
Some frosts or snow may change the scene,
Occasional sunshine in between
Interminable squalls of rain.

Daffodils show and catkins wave,
Fluorescent willow by the stream;
Rooks congregate in tall bare trees
And Lapwings "*peewit*" on the wing –
The signs are there, the runes to read
To tell us this is nearly Spring.

More evidence presents itself:
Forsythia's gold before the green
Of hedgerow leaves and celandines,
Pale primrose shiver in the breeze.
Then comes a day of gentle warmth,
The breeze has dropped, the sky is blue.

An early Brimstone takes to flight,
There's not a cloud to spoil the view
As spiralling lark begins to sing –
It's now we know that Winter's gone...
 And that today it's really Spring.

WILLOW

It was the first still day of Spring
I came across you by the lake.
For mirrored, lonely, lovely girl
It seemed a secret solitude –
A mood, perhaps, I should not break.

I watched you bending to the pool,
Bright celandines smiled up at you,
A princess letting down her hair
To rippling mirror of the mere
As breezes kissed the water there.

You are your loveliest in Spring -
So why be sad, why do you weep?
Most feminine of all the trees
Please let your tresses cascade down :
As crimped coiffure and verdant gown.

MAGICIANS

Here come the swallows
Wheeling over the bay,

Bringing African
Blue to replace the grey;

They are towing the sun
Home across the spray,

They are warming the land :
Starting summer today,

Surprising old crows and the secretive jay.

Here come the swallows
Swooping over the town -

Nesting in the barn
Behind the *Rose & Crown*;

They are spelling out
FREEDOM above the Downs;

They are conjuring shoots
Where the land is brown

And dressing Mother Earth
In a verdant gown.

GREEN AND PLEASANT

And as the spring unfolds it's there —
Hanging on air — pungent, sickly,
Bitter scent assaulting nose and throat
With every breath. Out travelling

This road — high hedged with windows shut
Up tight — it permeates the car :
I know the crop before that flash
Of lurid yellow proclaims *rape*.

Florescent acid yellow flames
Steal from laburnum's subtle spark —
And from the hills a patchwork glows —
An alien crop burns England's heart.

SALLOW

On Beltaine Day (this first of May)
The air outside is filled with snow :
Not like the cold of wintertime -

When flakes fall steadily to ground -
But this snow drifts, rises and falls
Then thickens with the passing breeze.

Through every window, open door,
The snow flows as it would in dreams :
Filling each ledge and entrance hall

With gossamer that floats away,
Evading house-proud, tidying hands.
Outside it catches leaves of plants,

Covering cobwebs and mown grass -
A snow scene under springtime sun.
So sallow willow sends its seeds

To ride the air like thistledown
Until a longed for shower of rain
Brings sweet relief and damps it down.

A WALK IN THE COUNTRY

The townies took a country walk
Upon a frosty day
They stopped to listen by the fence,
"A drum, a mile away."

The noise it sounded once again
A sudden distant "Crack!"
"I think it's getting closer dear,
Maybe we should turn back."

"Perhaps it is a poacher's gun"...
"Another way's worth trying"...
"I'm not sure we should've come.
"Why does he keep on firing?"

"It is a gun! - It's getting near!
Is it war or murder?"
Behind the hedge the farmer grins
And resets his bird scarer.

FLEDGLING AT WEST END

Rescued from our amiable cat,
The fledgling lay, cupped in your hands,
Eyes closed and struggling for breath,
Trembling with shock or close to death.

Out in the air, under blue skies -
The trees alive with song of birds -
It seemed to calm, stop trembling,
As fluttering, it looked around.

Then came that certain point in time :
It perched upon your fingertips -
We stood there willing it to go -
As it remembered how to fly.

Where do all those moments go
As present time becomes the past?
Who records those tears of joy,
Remarks upon each new bird's flight?

DEATH *of the* PHEASANT MAN

The view from Larkshill has now changed :
Near Ted Gale's farm, the *Pheasantry*
Is packing up. Down come the arcs,
Where hens had grown from lively chicks.
Stacked in neat rows : heaters, feeders,
Paraphernalia and odd bits
Accumulated over time.

Soon, netting fences will be gone,
The stock sold on and anything
Not saleable will all be burnt.
His sons work hard to clear the site
Not wanting to take on a life
Uncertain and so seasonal.

Last to be moved, his caravan -
Moss green with weather, on seized wheels -
Where he stayed warm on cool Spring nights.
And to this field return mute hens,
Escapees searching for a mate,
Surprised to find this man has gone.

And, as the shadow's fingers creep
Across the grass towards the east,
A flock of doves circle this field
Marking the evening of his sleep.

SUMMER RAIN

(Haiku)

Across the window
Hang long strings of heavy jewels :
Raindrops on snail trails.

RICHES

In summertime the poorest child
Has shoes deep gilded like a king's :
Yellow - gold from meadow flowers -
To dancing feet a fortune clings.

WARFIELD VISITOR

Straightening up while edging grass,
I spotted him as I stood up -
Red Kite above the Home Farm Woods.
Catching the sun, he blazed fox red -
Magnificent his circling -
Till, with a flick of his forked tail
He caught the breeze to head north-west.
Like nylon kites above Larkshill,
This bird is tethered to its home :
A pull, like Ariadne's thread,
Will draw him back to Beacon Hill
And Cowleaze Wood in distant Bucks.

CROWS

Still moonshine.
A chatter of crows
Prelude celebration of first light.
Whilst others sleep
These shadows caw across the stubbled field :
Black harbingers who come with tales of death.

ON CABBAGE HILL

(Watching Deer)

At dusk, from off the bank
Where primroses had been,
We watched for wary shades :
Deer, inching through the wheat.

Excitement carefully checked,
We froze and dared not breath
As antlered heads bobbed close
Across that golden sea.

Thrilling to see them near -
Elusive and so shy -
A tingle like the time
We watched kingfishers dive.

We waited silently
As night began to fall :
Dogs barked, a cow lowed once,
Wind rippled ripening corn.

Not deer - but being with you,
Is what I most recall :
The closeness of our wait,
Our hearts beating as one;

A tiny sense of hope,
A symbol of our love.

ONE OF THOMPSON'S BOYS

Picture this :

A perfect summer afternoon,
The flowers in bloom, striped chairs on grass
Beneath the shading apple tree.

Out of the blue, a strange white cloud
Descends : drifting, eddying smoke,
Covering grass, flowers, trees

Engulfing cottages and cars.
And when it's gone, what's left is strange :
A winter scene - part dusted white.

Whilst, in the field beyond the lane,
A tractor drags its cloud of lime
Away from cottages and cars

And up the hill towards the gate,
The driver whistling tunelessly -
Job done, no worries, time for tea.

SEPTEMBER

Solitary, the robin sits
And hears the apple's muffled fall;
In twos white butterflies persist
With fading buddleia by the wall.

Though air is cooling, still the sun
Keeps insects busy round the flowers
And we can laze where water runs,
Rejoicing in these stolen hours.

WINDFALLS

In this, the Autumn of her life,
Windfalls.
Mossed tree - planted to mark her birth -
Has grown too tall,
With fruit too high to reach.
Each day she waits for wind and sun
To bring her windfalls down.

And life has always been like this -
Spent tending to the fallen fruit :
Both parents, husband, then her son
Had tumbled from the family tree,
Been rescued after falling low
Like windfalls - bruised but whole.

HARVEST

Beneath trees heavy with fruit :
An apple, discarded in the grass,
Crimson, yellow streaked, speckled.
Viewed from this side, spherical and whole.
Here magical deception :
Fruit beguiles the eye but not the hand.
No solidity, weightless;
Leathery, light of skin : an empty husk.

Tree born, the apple endured
Through June when Codling caterpillar
Bored a home in this fruit's heart.
To the grass it fell, tiny grubhole
Soon enlarged as probing birds
Hunt moth's pink offspring. Crisp juiciness
Now exposed, white apple flesh
Attracts the earwig and wasp; the ants
Complete the job of stripping
To the skin this apple in the grass :
Crimson, yellow streaked, speckled.
Viewed from this side, spherical and whole.

QUELM LANE

Quelm lane has changed : surfaced and firm -
No longer haunt, by Bulbrooke's field,
For ghostly rider and white horse -
It's now the place to walk the dog.

Part flanked by Bracknell's overspill,
It still connects to a green past
Where muddied hounds from Garth Hunt's pack
Splashed through deep puddles, homeward bound.

Today, beneath the changing trees,
A fox, unbothered by the past,
Strolls down the lane towards Larks Hill -
Aware, behind, I'm closing fast.

He shows no fear : is unaware
Today's the day that hunting starts,
His only danger lurks on roads -
Round here he's safe to lead his life.

I pedal faster but he's gone -
Dissolving through the blackthorn hedge;
I ride through Quelm Lane's falling leaves -
He's off to check the farm for eggs.

OCTOBER MAPLE

Red - gold, it burns across first frosted grass,
Maple, requiting Summer's alchemy.

Commutable : against a perfect blue
Transposed - the Autumn sun's epitome.

HORSE CHESTNUTS IN OCTOBER

From green to gold, from red to brown
Horse chestnut leaves come spiralling down;
These waving hands applaud the sun -
Summer's demise, Autumn begun.

AUTUMN SUNDAY, BERKSHIRE

(Mohammed visits Warfield)

Before the sun had warmed these Berkshire fields,
As first birds stirred and local traffic slept;
While horses stood like statues by the stream
And diamonds jewelled tall grass and each cobweb;
Before the congregation rose for church
And tired dog walkers tumbled from their beds;
An unseen stranger ambled village roads,
Passed sleeping houses and *The Yorkshire Rose.*

Wandering down the narrow forded lane,
Along a bridleway of hips and haws,
He found a gateway, set back off the track
And, book in hand, he intoned silent prayers.
In solitude he watched the rising sun
While every local body was at rest,
'Though no one else gave thanks for this new day -
The only man at prayer ignored the west.

NOT AN ODE TO AUTUMN

Only crab apples on the trees;
A cold wind blows across the lease
Stirring the spent brown leaves that cling
Where just the jaunty robin sings.
Late Autumn mists can quickly hide
All vestige of sun, moon and tide.
In leafless woods and barren fields
The future slowly disappears :
On Autumn days that bring despair
A chill of death hangs in the air.

My mind has seen the seasons round
But Autumn has me trapped and bound.

Written as a response to "Ode to Autumn" by John Keats.

Lease = dialect for open pasture or common land.

NOT ALL IT SEEMS

(Haiku)

Stumbling from my bed,
I'm sleep-blind in white moonlight :
Look! The moon makes snow.

AUTUMN FIND

(Haiku)

On this bush a bag :
Wind blown polythene, here to
Put our blackberries in.

WINTER SOLSTICE, WARFIELD

All night the village gleamed with lights.
By dawn the chase and flash have stilled,
Neon dimmed, the glitter gone.
Now, in cold brightness, trees look sad :
Cable-bound, wreathed with dead-eyed lamps,
They wait, impatient for the night.

On Larkshill orchard trees were decked -
An Advent custom now revived -
But gales have swept the tinsel down,
Spread broken streamers on the grass,
Leaving the orchard looking bleak -
As festive as the Longshot tip.

Trees are best dressed without man's help :
At West End Farm, where horses wait
In icy fields, in solitude,
Crab apples hang above the gate,
Sparkling, frosted, on cold air :
Gold Christmas baubles catching sun.

LORD ORMATHWAITE'S ROUGH MUSIC

(The Ballad of Warfield Park)

This tale from Warfield's history
Is, perhaps, the most bizarre :
Of the second Lord Ormathwaite
And a night that was ill-starred.

Arthur Benn Walsh was this lord's name -
The Baron of Warfield Park -
Confronted by a village mob
In the deep October dark.

Arthur'd married a sweet young wife -
Somerset's Emily Kate,
Her kindness to the villagers
Had them queuing at her gate.

During that time of hardship, when
The poor were really in need,
Emily won their hearts and minds
Through charity and good deeds.

It was back in seventy-four,
In Queen Victoria's reign,
Rumour ran wild in the parish
That Emily was in pain.

It seemed that domineering lord
Would often mistreat his wife-
Feelings raged high in the village,
Hearing of Emily's strife.

They plotted in the old *New Inn*
And in the *Plough & Harrow* :
The talk was all of "*Skimmy Rides*"
Instead of growing marrows.

"What that man needs is a lesson,
We need to cause him some pain -
If we give 'im a good tinnin'
'E might start usin' 'is brain."

"Get pots and pans and old tin cans
An' a whacker - like a stick,
We'll deafen that louse Ormathwaite
When we play our Rough Music."

So off they marched passed Horsenaile's House
Shouting and making a din,
"We're off to see Lord Ormathwaite
To repent 'im of 'is sins."

Four hundred trekked to Warfield Park
Where they marched around the Hall,
Arthur was finishing dinner
When his neighbours came to call.

The Baron rushed to the window -
Leaving his half finished meal,
Fury and anger took over :
Stormed out to face his ordeal.

"Quiet, you rabble!" he shouted -
The music suddenly stilled,
The mob faced up to his ranting -
The air now suddenly chilled.

"I know your face Thomas Butler,
I know you Harry the Smith -
Don't try to hide Robert Bowyer -
You're standing by young Griffith."

Those at the back were now restless,
Someone let out a loud moan,
Suddenly up the band started -
Cheering, they headed for home.

The *tinners'* triumph was short lived -
Twenty-nine summonses came,
Calling them to Wokingham court -
These few to carry the blame.

But Arthur soon left the parish -
Slunk to his holding in Wales,
Ormathwaites ended up bankrupt -
Put their Park home up for sale.

Ghosts don't forget the harsh treatment
Of those poor men who once erred...
Sometimes, on dark Autumn evenings,
Rough Music still can be heard.

FOOTNOTE

One of the most alarming rural traditions was known as the
Skimmington Ride, Ran Tanning, Riding the Stang, Tinning or *Rough Music.*
When a man was exposed as having been unfaithful to his wife or
shown to have ill-treated her, a mob of neighbours would gather
together to shout, beat frying pans, saucepans or anything that would
make a noise. Often an effigy of the offending husband was made.
The mob, effigy in tow, would make their noisy way around the
village to the house of the offender where the effigy would be burnt.
The Mayor of Casterbridge, Thomas Hardy's novel of 1886, describes
such a *Skimmington Ride.*

ONCE IT'S GONE, IT'S GONE

(WARFIELD)

See the Larks Hill owls blinking down from boxed security,
They're clinging on like West End bats, huddled under eaves,
They're looking at a changing land where once they could fly free.

Last chance for the old farmhouse left marooned in Abbey Place,
New homes will fill the golden fields where once the horses grazed,
Soon garage and its yellow trucks are set to be replaced.

They're calling time at Battle Bridge, cars rusting in the yard,
The orange glow from by-pass road illuminates the night
Where young bikers and joy riders scream by with disregard.

They'll soon bring in new families to live where deer have fed,
Tarmac over ancient ways and grub up half the hedge with
Its insects and its flowers – once all the birds have fled.

Goodbye to the quiet life of the peaceful country lanes,
They'll shoe-horn in more houses, keep this copse – dog walking space,
But land that just grows houses is marked by the curse of Cain.

A place named in the Doomsday Book to a suburb of *that* town,
Losing its land and history if tarmac is rolled out,
Under brick the meadowland will drown in that ugly brown.

Old ways will be forgotten without protest and debate,
Remember the name while it matters – ancient Saxon place,
It could become just a sign on a road flanked by big estates.

Other Places, Other Faces

MOTORWAY EPIPHANY

Road, chosen for convenience,
Used for our journeys heading west,
Is not a stimulating drive.

So trees become a talking point -
A punctuation for each ride -
A measure for the passing time.

These acres would be hard to miss :
Spruce, tidy in neat graded rows,
March up a slope and out of sight.

Grown on this scale to satisfy
Tradition from Victorian times,
Each tree must reach a standard height.

November brought the harvesting :
Trees cut and bagged and stacked by size,
Were organised by lorry loads.

Today the scent of burning pine
Wafts slowly over carriageways,
Smoke, like a veil across the trees,
Marks passing of this Christmas time.

BLIGHTED SPRING

At Chapel Farm they're left without a prayer :
The signs are up to show *NO RIGHT OF WAY,*
A hundred years of milking ends today.

Across the valley nothing moves but smoke :
Gone, suckling ewe that answered to her name,
Redundant dogs now skulk the yard in vain.

The midday fox, unharried on his way,
Halts in Home Meadow, unconcerned by man,
To puzzle at the silence of these lambs.

AT PRACTICE

(April Surfers, Exmouth)

Where rain lies white as mist
Upon a steel grey sea,
They wait the rising waves -
These bobbing, neoprene seals.

Between timed wiper blades
We watch their rise and fall;
Like twitchers in a hide,
We huddle in our car.

Spray blows from each wave cap
Beyond the crashing surf
That scours the naked beach :
Boiling an orange-red.

In turn they ride these crests :
Harnessing speed and power,
Fleetingly to stand erect
Before their waves crash down.

Braving the wind and cold
They're driven by a dream :
Golden sands, the perfect tan
And a place on the surfing scene.

COTSWOLD VIEW

Where sheep once grazed, the town has grown :
Cheap terraces crawl up the hill,
An overspill that planners planned –
Another eyesore pays the bills.

This valley sees another tide
Of buildings stretching from the town,
Industrial parks and service roads
Reach out towards the distant downs.

Greed is the spur to rip the land,
To tear out minerals from below;
To gouge the hills and mine the fields
And take the home of fox and crow.

Beyond this rise the land is safe :
Farmed and cared for down the years;
Viewed from afar, from distant hills,
Mosaic of fields and woods is clear.

Protected for a thousand years
These hills and valleys are unchanged
No infill, quarry, house or road
This view will ever disarrange.

Yet recently a change has come
Promoted by the farmers here:
"An innocent reuse of land -
A different crop should not be feared."

Soon acres of fluorescent growth
On each farm dominates the scene,
The country's raped by oil seed -
A yellow sea which once was green.

And now the view from here has changed
Dramatically in so few years,
Over valleys, plains, distant hills
Bright fields of rape have soon appeared.

But that's not all, more sinister
Is how rape spreads by hand unseen :
Wind blown for miles from farmer's fields
The seeds, like snow fall in a dream,

Seems now to be most everywhere,
Out of control it will succeed
In covering every inch of land
Till nothing shows but oil seed.

VIEW WITH A KILL

Here, autumn skies are blue as spring
And valleys dress in burnished gold.

Red ahead - traffic slowing up.
A ditch bound car and knot of men
Sign accident to travellers.
A huntsman on a skittish mare
Tetchily waves the traffic on.
Farmers and horses crowd the verge,
Hounds keen beyond the broken hedge.

And down the road, two fields away,
A fox lopes on towards the sun.

VALLEY OF THE KITES

Beneath a pure November sky
Kites give perspective to a view
Across towards the Oxford Plain.
From Beacon Hill we watched them glide
Then spiral upwards in a sky
So blue, above the motorway,
Where tarmac breeches Chiltern chalk.

Above cocooned dull travellers
They surf the air-waved diesel thrum
Till tail flicks set them off again,
Away from traffic fumes and noise
Towards the trees of Cowleaze Wood.
And here, south of the motorway,
The natural silence is restored.
Below Bald Hill the valley runs
With banks of juniper and scrub.
Unchanged in years, a special place,
The chosen home for these Red Kites.

Our giant, russet, gliding birds
Join others in a group of four
To search and quarter valley floor,
Aware of movement from great height.
And, in the distance, other groups
Of Kites are doing just the same :
Spiralling as they rise and fall,
Then swoop away, begin again.

So, mesmerised, we watched for hours
With only sheep for company;
As time stood still, we had returned
Like strangers to an ancient land -
Seeing the landscape as it was,
Brought back in time by rufous Kites.

*Once common across England, the Red Kite was persecuted
to near extinction by the end of the 19th. Century.
In 1989 a re-introduction programme brought Red Kites back
To theChilterns. There are now over 200 breeding pairs in
Southern England.*

ROME

Japan is empty now! In every shot
Themselves - with Rome a backdrop to their time
On tour. Each monument becomes a dot,
An adjunct to their transient joy, no rhyme
Or thought for beauty's past or ancient place
While they have cameras, smiles and Gucci bags.

And would *The Steps* still be to John Keats' taste?...
This scrum of souls with all their national flags,
Costly, must have brands, posing - looking hot,
Trying to be cool - waiting for a sign
Of fabled *fifteen minutes fame* that's not
Unlike *name writ in water* - not sublime
Like Keats's modest phrase - but more germane
To media fed obsessions that obtain...

PENSION DAY

After the weekly pilgrimage
There's time to kill before the bus.
Slowly, with sticks and bags they come,
Following decal walkway signs
Which point them to *Café Revive*.
It's here these grey haired waiters wait,
Like patients at a surgery,
Sitting, heads bowed, on hard-backed chairs
Each with a coffee or sweet tea -
They stretch each minute, sip their drinks.
Close by ironic signs declare :
End of the Line and *Last few Days*,
A joke that they refuse to see -
They sit and fiddle with their cups.

Time drags so slowly sitting here -
Each week, another *Groundhog Day* -
Yet do some wish to break the mould?…
To ride without a travel pass
And make a journey, not by bus.

PARADOX

I have imagined her
peering short sightedly
through steam
tutting, *"It can't be me!"*
"Those lines and bags
and yet I feel eighteen."

Today's another day …
wiping the glass,
my father's face aflame.
"It can't be me,
I haven't changed!" -
Inside I'm still the same.

How does it happen?
We all take care :
avoid the risks,
make nothing change...
Yet time and life are dangerous -
when suddenly it comes to this.

THE READING TEST

It takes an age for you to move
From Blue Badged car to waiting chair :
Those alien legs refuse to work —
Leave you tottering on the brink
Of actual or imagined falls...

But today's visit is for eyes
At Opthalmology — First Floor.
You brave the lift — there is no choice —
And soon you're wheeled into a room
With lights and lenses, screens and lists.

A grey haired woman, half your age,
Conducts the tests that measure sight
And sits to hear you read from books.
"Try this ...and this...Well done!" she says,
Marking success with ready praise

As you had done those years before
When you had taught her class to read.

FROM GRID REFERENCE : 60   *(moving west)*

On looking back from here, all's clear and bright :
Fresh sunshine bathes the valley floor with light,
Each hill and copse now holds that golden glow
Of challenges surpassed along the way.

Rough places on the path seem simply smooth,
And detours can be seen round barriers
Found hard to cross. See : where I ran, or walked
Or limped - It's good to rest and heal these bumps.

Looking ahead, the view is not so clear -
I only see a few steps up the way.
I'll take advice from travellers gone before
On pitfalls, routes and mileage for each day.

Refreshed, still in good shape, but slower now,
Climbing again, I'm taking up the slack -
I'll move with caution (and a lighter pack)
Into the mists, where friendly voices call.

DEATH OF A PRINCESS

A gulf between us based on privilege -
A life, always ruled by the great divide,
For you, every day rolled serenely by -
From here it seemed the easiest of rides.

Now private staff perform their last goodbyes
And dogs are not allowed into the hall;
Security discretely melts away,
A guard of honour - but no bugle calls.

The single piper sends you on your way
In borrowed limousine you slowly glide;
Along the route bare headed, silent crowds,
But at the gates outriders leave your side.

Now stripped of class, you're moving on alone,
At last, in death, you find the common touch :
Your place is booked to join the patient queue
And feed the flames - just like the rest of us.

Princess Margaret was cremated at Slough crematorium.

PAUSE

Silently he appeared,
Eeling through bushes and the hedge.
He was magnificent :
Russet, amber, red -
And all around was stilled.
Pausing, he shrank the view -
Till all we saw was fox.

Just watching him helped slow your tears
And stopped your thoughts of death.

EASTER MOON

Easter retains remembered suffering :
Always a time for faith — when love hurts.

Now, host like, a full moon slowly rises.
It's no cliché this — just a bitter pill —

This moon-breast rising on an x-ray screen
With a shadow — a cloud — like an eclipse :

Easter retains remembered suffering.

TURNINGS

On sullen days like these I wake,
Wondering where I went so wrong :
Only nine lives and seven gone -
So, how do I get to heaven?

Brooding, an outcast in the rain,
Feeling helpless - love's taken flight -
Yet somehow miracles occur :
Snowdrops in Arctic winds unfurl;
Migrating birds are soon in sight;
Insects buzz as fruit forms on the vine.

Then there are evenings after heat :
Warm, slow breezes under stars;
Late summer days with dew on grass,
When cobwebs gleam with precious jewels;
The high flung hopeful song of larks,
Rising above a gusting wind…

And so, like this, I learn to live :
Heart opens like a rose past rain
As sun comes streaming through again
With birdsong in a shower of notes.

50s INCIDENT

"We always had to make our own amusement.."

A stranger staying down our road
(Visiting with his favourite aunt)
Had gained respect from local kids
By telling tales of things he did.
His railway trick was new to me
And, on those boring summer days,
Any excitement seemed like fun.

Up the embankment by the bridge
Where tracks ran straight for several miles,
We kept down low and out of sight
Of the Nine Elms signal man.
Hidden by scrub & buddleia
We inched our way close to the tracks
Where distance shimmered in the heat.

"I've only ever tried with two,"
Our new friend said - but we were three -
Each with a penny to squash flat
Beneath a hundred wheels of steel.
But what if three was one too much -
Causing the train to jump the track?
At ten we were too curious
To worry much about that stuff.
So, one by one, we inched our way
From cover to the railway tracks -
Three pennies shining in the sun,
Together on the outside line.

We waited for what seemed an age
Crushed deep into embankment grass
Until we heard the signal *clang* -
A green light for our down line train.
There was a singing from the track,
Then it came rushing through the haze
A laden coal train from the north
Towing a billow of black smoke.
Too late to change our minds and run,
We pressed our hearts into deep grass
As yards away the train charged passed,
Crashing and screeching near our heads.
The earth shook with each passing truck
As time was torn by flying wheels,
Then, suddenly, the noise was gone :
Fading to a distant click.

Summer returned and insects buzzed.
Somehow the rest all seemed a blur :
Stumbling up across the lines,
Hunting amongst the ballast stones -
The red faced, shouting signal man -
Racing across four sets of tracks
And laughing all the way back home.

NO DEVILS OR ANGELS

At a time
Between
Waking and dreams,
Games and girls,
Poetry came.
No memories
Of day or place :
No devils or angels;
Like walking at night
Or a waking dream
Is all I recall…

And my thoughts
Marshalled,
And a rhythm
Like a pulse.
It was a calling :
Coming out of clear air,
Taking me from the others,
With fire in my eyes
But no passion or pain.

I had lost my Self -
Then it touched me.

POETRY MATTERS

Old slipper wearing pessimist
Had mentioned, when he wrote of Yeats :
"Poetry makes nothing happen…"
And , in the greater scheme of things
He's right…No poem ever stilled
The guns, prevented war, or stopped a fight.
But poems work as epitaphs;
Become the pillows for our dreams,
Gather us up when times are rough :
Provide a comfort, sooth our needs.
Poems can conjure life or death,
Daffodils or a thrush in spring;
Poems have room for all mankind -
From beauty to the kitchen sink;
Whether in free verse or in rhyme,
The good ones always make you think.

"In Memory of W.B.Yeats" W.H.Auden famously wrote :
"Poetry makes nothing happen…"

BIOGRAPHER

The desk had been the focus of her life -
The place to write and organise her time;
Just like the way she structured every day,
Her filing had a rhythm and a rhyme.
Behind the will, & list of stocks and shares,
I found a file, simply marked, *"Biography,"*
Easily missed among receipts and bills....
Could this file be my great discovery?

Holding piles of paper - folded scraps -
Well marshalled and in order like her bills,
Each item helped to document her life -
Right down to medication for her ills.
Old snapshots seemed to hint at a romance -
But nothing else here spoke of true love's ways -
Just briefest notes of families' births and deaths,
Of visits, visitors and holidays.

The rest concerned her writing : dates and times,
Struggles, successes and her publishers;
But little of this told of how she felt
Or of any things that gave her pleasure.
Could this, then, be the total of a life?
(Clues, perhaps, embedded in her poetry?)
If she'd been a lover or a wife
I'd be writing more than just a history.

STILL

He was to be their special gift :
Miracle child - conceived in failing hope -
Perfect in the deep dark of the scan.
He was complete, more than they dared believe :
An elfin, smiling face and hands that waved -
As if he watched them from that silver screen.

Reports were fine : an active growing child
Whose tiny bird-like heart beat strong.

One summer dawn he came -
When birds were hushed and all was still -
And he came perfect to this world :
Born sleeping - as time arrests
And nature seemed to catch her breath.

(A reflection on a churchyard memorial)

HER DIAMOND MAN

Ashes turned into diamonds.
A US firm says it will turn your cremated ashes into a diamond
for the loved ones you leave behind.   BBC NEWS 22/08/02

Employed as nurse, she soon became
Companion in those empty days
When family said they had no time.
She quickly found new ways to please,
Catering to his every need
And learnt to ask about the past.
He told about his diamond days -
The deals & how a fortune's made -
His squabbling wives & children's greed.

Constant companion, bright new friend,
She soon was indispensable.
On summer walks she took his arm
And wore short shorts - he loved her legs -
And she became his *Golden Girl.*
She laughed and said, *"Dear Daniel,*
Then you must be my Diamond Man."
Such happy days - but, oh, so brief -
For suddenly, he up and died.

The family were outraged - the will had changed -
Soon got their lawyers & the press engaged :
Young totty more than companion
To octogenarian diamond baron...
But, after all the fuss, she still shone through.

The new life style, she'd taken in her stride,
But something deep inside was missing him.
Surfing the net one day she found
"LifeGem ...the perfect way to embrace
Your loved one's memory day by day" -
"How neat, and so appropriate."
So now she feels he's very close -
A friend still giving good advice -
As glinting from her pinky ring
He's there to point her way in life.

FEBRUARY 14th.

Look at the pictures on this calendar :
It is the perfect day on *Kiribati,* *
The sky a seamless blue and azure sea
Where men go out to fish as all men must.

Here small lagoons are made as heart shaped traps :
Each heart a triumph for the waller's hand -
Meticulously formed from piled stone -
With one small gap where fish swim over sand.

In England's cold I face your heart of stone
And hope this day to find that secret gap
Where, eel like, love can find the only way
Into your heart, inside love's tender trap.

* Pronounced : *kee-ree-bus*

KIRIBATI is an island nation of coral atolls in the Pacific Ocean.

TONIGHT'S THE NIGHT

Reaching her through vanity works best :
Remember, first admire her eyes or hair,
Always praise the shoes or clothes she wears -
If all else fails, let flowers do the rest.

Your average bloke enjoys girls with big tits,
Lad's nights out & lie-ins on a Sunday;
To please him, keep his belly filled with chips -
Just thank God he's back to work on Monday.

Obsession with his car may make you sick,
But reaching him means talking cams and gears;
He'll talk the torque then buff up his *Goodyears*
But, without wheels, he's just a little prick.

Some girls compete as if they're really blokes :
Driving fast and getting smashed on Fridays;
They can be yours for just one line of coke :
The challenge - taking risks - will make them stay.

Old rock stars with pathetic pony tails,
Fierce piercing, naff tattoos and balding heads,
Seem to have a need for teenage girls -
To feed their egos : in and out of bed.

Short ugly men get more than their fair share
Of women who look best when they're undressed -
These tarts don't see the wrinkles these men wear
As it's money, power, status they like best.

Old totty with her toyboy on her arm
Believes that she's *The Face* this *Ladies Day*.
He's such a catch : his looks, that grace and charm -
Behind her back he mocks her 'cause he's gay.

PERSONAL EFFECTS

We found it hidden in a box,
An unmarked tape tucked casually
Between weddings and birthday snaps.
The family always used to laugh
About the hours and hours he'd shot
Of everyone and everywhere
Without a second of himself -
"Too busy being camera man,"
Was what he said in his defence -
Yet here it was : two minutes worth
Of film devoted to himself.

Shot with set focus - the camera fixed -
There is enough to show the world
He takes his pleasure seriously,
While brazen, giggling girls
Take turns -
Enjoy a joke at his expense...

That was the thing we hated most...

ADAM AS ENTREPRENEUR

(To be read in a West Country Accent)

"Well," *Adam said, draining his pint,*
"That garden were real special, mind;
All them plants : trees of perfect fruit,
Flowers of every kind and just
Enough insects pollinatin.'
Climate like a glasshouse : sunny
Days, gentle rain at night - clockwork.
An' the soil - in all me days I've
Never seen the like - some gardener -
No wonder 'e called it *Eden.*
I was made up - with 'im askin'
Me to run it - just me and Eve….
In a place that could run isself.

Mind you, 'e 'ad is funny ways :
Regulashuns…that sort o' thing -
Tellin' us *"Don't eat that fruit"*, -
An' us livin' in a orchard!
Fact is 'e got peculiar,
Callin' this un his *Knowledge Tree* -
Its crabby fruit reserved for 'im.
Mind you, all this got me to think,
Wonderin' how I could taste his fruit
Without the need to take a bite.
He were quick enough telling' us
What not to do - but no advice,
No mention of that serpent's ways.
Of all the creatures livin' there,
IT was the worst. A real smoothy,
You should've seen 'im creep round God.

Anyway, once I had this dream -
All bright it was, about God's Tree :
By turnin' all the fruit to juice
I could avoid 'is stupid ban
'Bout eatin' it - a DRINK you see -
But first I'd 'ave to make a press
To squeeze the fruit down into juice.
I worked out how to do all this
Then went to tell the plan to Eve,
Unaware, as I hatched that plot,
Snake-in-the-grass heard every word.

So I went off to make the press -
No sooner than me back was turned
Old crawler's there, chattin' up Eve.
Like someone from a used car lot
Or travellin' salesman, door to door,
He's smarmin' round her with his guff....
Why is it women fall for words?
He told how apples kept God wise
And that me press would never work;
"*Go on*," he says, "*A little bite
Will do no harm & keep you bright.*"

I'd never heard God shout before -
Somehow he knew what Eve had done,
So, when I rushed back 'ome to 'er
God's there waitin - we're showed the door.
Mind you, the press worked perfect, like
And it come with us when we left.
We've made our fortune overnight
With cider, perries and the rest;
But I can't get the apples right -
They taste like God's, but fail the test :
No drinker's gained in knowledge yet -
They all gets drunk and just forgets.

Go on then, right, make mine a pint.

SEEING THE LIGHT

(Pass me that axe, Eugene)

"Home security lighting emits a harsh, intrusive
and environmentally unfriendly light that is
often a serious nuisance to neighbours. ..."
(The Chartered Institute of Environmental Health)

Lost in a coracle of dreams
I bob the night away between
The shores of wakefulness and sleep.
Outside the rain lashes the roof
And windswept trees sway to and fro
Like a green sea. The neighbour's light
Is triggered by this restless tide
And, lighthouse like, it sends its beams
Across the darkness to my dreams -
Dragging me back from storm tossed sleep.
Hardly awake, but not at rest,
I doze until the gusting wind
Sets off the trees and starts the light.
I toss and turn till darkness comes
Then, reaching borders of my dreams,
The light comes on again... again...
This lasts till dawn when natural light
Extinguishes those piercing beams;
The wind has dropped, the rain has stopped
And for an hour I'm left to sleep
Till tired out and bleary eyed
I rise to face a taxing day.
Late in to work, a colleague jeers
About my candle's burning ends,
"I wish it was as good as that,"
I grumble, making up my mind
The light or trees will have to go...

When measuring security
Those thrashing trees are no great risk,
And there is never any need
To light each passing fox or cat -
Perhaps my neighbour will see sense...

If not, pass me that axe, Eugene...

THE KNACK

(For T.H.)

Looking across the net
He knew the way the kid would feel.
He had been there himself :
Knowing no fear,
Ebullient and self possessed -
Riding his strength and skill.
Hunger, ambition, arrogance
Fuelled his success -
Then he could sleep at night :
Confident and best.

His time has come. His body aches.
The proud flame that drives him on
Evaporates.
Clothes cling with sweat,
Sweat stings his eyes -
Trapped in a cauldron of heat and noise.

Over the net, the young boy's
Features change as he pictures there
Faces of champions he's played.
In silence he focuses his will.
Playing from memory -
Of aces from the past -
He winds up, refreshed :
Serving for the match.

BALLAD FOR THE BELFAST BOY

The first time we saw Georgie
He was just a skinny kid
Brought in for the missing Babes
We remember what he did -

He was the man…

His footwork was audacious -
He could leave a team for dead -
Defenders were bamboozled
As he scored with foot or head -

Played like a dream…

He soon became top scorer
And the *Player of the Year,*
When he'd turned just twenty-two
He was better than his peers -

He was the Best!

He found a lot of new friends
And the ladies loved his eyes -
He built himself a new home
But there was no where he could hide -

He was a star…

He started missing training
And the press were on his case :
Reporting on his love life,
All that clubbing , such a waste -

He did it all…

So he found himself a secret
Way to keep on feeling high -
He didn't need a dentist's chair,
George was rarely ever dry -

Drink was his friend...

His fame brought many changes
And the vultures came to call,
Like Greavesie he hit benders
But he didn't need a ball -

Life was a blur...

The King grew fat in Vegas
While the Beatles came undone -
All those swinging days were ending
And the end had just begun -

George walked away...

He tried to stop his drinking
And to be his charming self;
The wagon left without him -
Found a bottle on the shelf -

Bringing him down...

Last place we saw Georgie
Was a tabloid photograph :
*Look and see what drink has done
As it stole away my life...*

Shankley was right!

Pundits replayed his talents,
Critics remembered the booze,
Fans recalled a complex man
Who always hated to lose…

Hated to lose…

And how the fans applauded
As they crowded his home ground,
Tribute to a genius,
On a banner, written down :

Simply the Best …
                    Georgie was Best.

PUSHING THE BOAT OUT...

Always one to make dramatic gestures,
Nelson is famed for *turning his blind eye*
And flagging up his famous expectations.

Less well known is his show for other ranks :
With just one arm he had to find a way
To treat his mess mates to expensive port.

A silver ship was wrought that ran on wheels
And in this strange device he kept his drinks.
So with extravagance Horatio showed

How to impress his men and play *mine host;*
Single handed he kept things on a roll :
Having a good time by *pushing out the boat.*

Nelson's silver ship is kept at Lloyds of London.

SONG (What Progress?)

See the deer glide by
Ghostly as a dream –
Dapple shades flicker through the hedge.

Moved here long before
Saxon hunters came,
They've stayed on to roam these woods and fields.

This country was green
Before the houses came,
The traffic roars
And roads glint in the rain,

Hard hats are worn,
They've brought the diggers in –
Concrete and bricks are down the lane.

Tick-tock
Goes the Snug Bar clock,
The village is set to change;

Ding-dong
Chime the old church bells,
Sunset falls across the waiting fields.

Meadows turning gold
Baking in the sun,
Empty now, waiting to be sold.

"Climate change is here"
Keeps running through my head –
We won't forget what Prescott said :
"Build at higher densities
On brownfield sites" –
SEERA plans for greenfield land
Just can't be right.

They're ripping out the hedge
Down on Crazies' Farm –
Morning traffic's backing up for miles.

Swallows congregate
Like beads on a wire –
Wonder whether they'll be back again?

Tick-tock
Goes the Snug Bar clock,
The village is set to change;

Ding-dong,
Ancient village bells
Sound a knell across the lonely fields.

When this place was young –
Just birds and trees and sun –
Before all the houses came,

People worked the land
Kept such a simple plan –
They valued life, everything they'd got.

Somewhere a councillor
Sprawls in an easy chair
Behind a big polished desk,

The houses on the hill
Were such an easy kill –
He took his money,
Signed up with the rest.

Tick-tock
Goes the Snug Bar clock,
The village is set to change;

Ding-dong
Play the wedding bells –

That this couple stay…

Sees the deer on their way.

Acknowledgements to N.Y.

NOT AUBADE

I leave you to untroubled sleep…

Rising in darkness, wide awake -
Alert as if it was midday -
Petty concerns have seen off sleep.
The demons who disturbed my rest
Will not be stilled whilst lying here
And make a racetrack in my head.

Calmed by dimmed light and humming fridge
My thoughts are slowed, I take control
And find solutions instantly
For silly problems that stole sleep.
The cats sleep curled like tight white balls
And through the window, endless dark
Envelopes trees and fields and hills.

A solitary car roars past,
Tunnelling night with lights and noise -
Going to where?… Leaving a tryst?
Or off to work the graveyard shift? -
A change of gears and up the hill,
It fades into the settled night.
And are there others at this hour
Who, like me, can find no rest?
And what of all those lonely souls
Who'll leave tonight , but will not rise?

Perhaps it's Larkin's demon death
Who troubles me and makes me wake,
Needing the darkness to commune...
Enough of this, it's back to bed,
For these thoughts do not frighten me -
Knowing I've left my own small mark
And found a love to last my life.

Clear headed now I watch you sleep
Then settle down and close my eyes.

WILD RANSOMS

Along the cliff edge -
Too far to safely reach -
These white bells tantalised
With their strange scent :
A pungent odour on the breeze
Their signature.

Later, in Roseland,
We saw them grown like weeds :
Filling meadows, smothering hedgerow grass,
Covering the roadside verge
Like gentle drifts of snow.

And at St. Just, filling the churchyard there,
Bluebells and ransoms like a haze
On every bank, round ancient graves.

And, through the palm
That grows where you now rest,
A solitary ransom flower had set.

Though far away in miles and time,
The smell of garlic takes me back -
Transports me instantaneously
To that Spring day :
The tiny church, the muddy creek,
The ransom flowers and you.